D1240114

HAPPY PILLZ

25 Tools to Overcome Overwhelm in Your
Everyday Life Amidst Normalcy OR Chaos

Jackie Minchillo

Copyright © 2020 Jackie Minchillo

All rights reserved

This book is based on the personal experience of the author and is not intended to provide medical advice.

No part of this book may be reproduced, or stored in a retrieval system, or transmitted in any form or by any means, electronic, mechanical, photocopying, recording, or otherwise, without express written permission of the publisher.

ISBN-13: 9780578780344

Cover design by: Agnesa Mahalla - Meha
Cover image by: Samba to the Sea Photography

Printed in the United States of America

To my angel Momma; my constant inspiration to
live in love. To my husband; my partner in chasing
dreams and my support system in the pursuance of
BEing better everyday. To my Uncle Ricky; may your
spirit live on to help others overcome their troubles.
To anyone who has wondered if there's someone out
there who 'understands'. You're not alone, xoxo

Contents

"Your path is more difficult because your calling is higher." -Unknown

LET'S GET ACQUAINTED...

The year is 2020, and it's overwhelming. A global pandemic hijacked life as we knew it, seemingly overnight. Racial inequality has come to yet another historic pinnacle and we have entire segments of our human population feeling less than and helpless in so many ways. We have more visibility than ever into the injustices that exist within a system built to "protect and guide" us. Political turmoil, worldwide, but particularly in the United States is at an all-time high. The lines between health and safety, morals and values, politics and propaganda, truth and opinion, reality and artificial construct are murkier than stagnant swamp water. And people, on the whole, are less tolerant than ever. Less tolerant of differences in all shapes and forms.

As a result of or in spite of (maybe a little of both) current events, our mental health crisis is worsening. The most recent aggregate data available is from 2018, and the American Foundation for Suicide Prevention reports suicide as the 10th leading cause of death in the United States. While final data won't be available until it's too late, experts across the globe are reporting historical, *staggering* numbers of suicides and suicidal thinking as a result of fear, social isolation and economic uncertainty in 2020. All on top of day-to-day life. Because being human is hard, even without our collective current state of affairs.

Sometimes overwhelm is hard to identify or articulate, let

alone admit. We live in a world that doesn't promote or support the sharing of raw emotion. A world that preaches we have the capacity to keep forging forward no matter what. And a world that views taking a step back to slow down, breathe and regroup as a sign of weakness.

The truth is, overwhelm is human nature whether it's popular to admit it or not. We all experience it. It's the broader springboard into sadness, anger, anxiety, fear, depression - all the things we ultimately experience when navigating and coping with our experience feels like "too much". A big exam, a big move, changing jobs, relationship upsets, death, grief, trauma, tragedy, a global pandemic, an increasingly intolerant social and political landscape, navigating working from home and homeschooling all while figuring out what the "truth" is in a sea of misinformation, lack of information and unnecessary information overload all at the same time... Was that a mouth full? That's OUR reality.

For as many beautiful things we each experience as a human BEing, the cycle of life demands we wade through the proverbial shit too. While it's how we learn and grow and know how to identify joy and love and fulfillment – it doesn't make it any less overwhelming at times.

I'm not a doctor. I'm not a life coach. I'm not a psychiatrist or therapist, and I'm not a grief or mental health "expert", not by any official capacity at least.

But the last decade has served me a series of experiences, all of which initially felt like some kind of unfair curse. I've managed somehow to hold onto to the deep belief, not the hallmark greeting card kind, but the real, gut-wrenching, sometimes painful and sometimes euphoric, innate understanding that everything TRULY happens for a reason. Even the bad, unfair, unjust, devastating, soul-shattering, mind-blowing stuff. It all serves a purpose, and I'm starting to come into that purpose in my own life, after years of being perplexed over the "why's?"

There has been so much of my personal journey I've never shared. Out of fear. Out of the deep conditioning that the positive stuff "sells" better. My own inner critic has run wild some days in writing this little book. "What qualifies YOU to give people advice to overcome overwhelm?"

When I say I'm coming into my purpose, part of what I mean is feeling called to share. We live in a share-obsessed society, yet most of what we share is cloaked in milestones, filters, presets and the notion that nobody has time to hear about our problems because they've got their own and "that's not what people want to read about". We're conditioned to believe that suffering in silence is better than burdening others. But what has saved me time and time again, when life became completely overwhelming, is connection. Finding someone who could relate. Real, authentic conversation. I'm not coming at this from a self-help soap box. Let me tell you a bit about where I'm coming from...

When I was 21, my grandfather and best friend took his last breath with his head in my lap on his garage floor after a freak fall. I had just gotten home (I was living with him at the time) and minutes before I arrived when I called to say I was on my way, he was just getting himself ready to take me to dinner.

I carried a deep, brutal sense of guilt over the timing of that day for a decade afterwards before I started to feel tangible healing taking place. Only recently, in 2020, sitting having a chat with my Grandpa's dear friend, an honorary grandmother to me who is 91 now, did I have a true epiphany. We were talking about that day and she said "You know he died happy right? He was so happy you were coming home to go to dinner; he literally died excited. It was quick, he didn't suffer. He hadn't lost his independence. He would've been miserable if he had. For those of us who know we're near the end, that's a dream. You know that, right?"

Would it have been so nice to have that perspective way earlier? Sure. But would I have been able to HEAR it? Internalize it? Know it to be true? Probably not. The timing is always perfect. But sometimes it takes us a long time to be *ready* for the messages we need.

At age 23, I learned why women who are victims of sexual assault/domestic violence and abuse oftentimes don't come forward through a toxic, manipulative, abusive relationship of my own. When I feared for my safety and had taken every possible measure I could to cut off contact, I turned to the authorities in an attempt to get a restraining order and was asked by the police "do you have physical proof that [this person] has physically harmed you or threatened your life?" What they meant was physical, current bodily evidence (or photos) or written proof in the form of a threat for example. If no, best of luck. The fact that I was being stalked and had the windows broken out of my car while I was at work was not enough. Too bad the security cameras in the parking lot were broken. They said "without proof it's your word against his." Being reminded by this person that he knew where I worked, where

I lived...was not enough. If I had nothing tangible to *show* them, they were not interested in my "word."

What I learned of our legal system (same with so many of our systems and institutions) is that we can expect reactionary help. But if you want to be proactive? Preventative? Protected? You're on your own. Who would feel supported? I know I didn't. I felt helpless. I felt ashamed. I felt scared.

Only now can I look back and see those same terrifying feelings fueled me. Motivated be to become stronger physically and mentally, to assure myself that another person would not make me feel helpless, ever again.

That same year, I stood by helplessly watching my Mom go through a manic, psychotic break and battle suicidal thoughts daily. I'll never forget the day she said to me, "honestly if it weren't for you, I probably would have been gone a long time ago." That's a heavy burden to bear, for anyone at any age. Not to mention, when you're looking at someone who is so loved and see they don't feel that love for themselves - it's a special kind of pain; one that shows you just how destructive our own mental prisons can be.

At age 25, just a few weeks before we were supposed to move into our first place together, my now husband's apartment building burned to the ground in a total loss fire in the dead of a Michigan winter, taking with it all of his Earthly possessions down to his coat and car keys. It also took most of my possessions I had been storing there including sentimental items like childhood mementos and photos. We ended up moving into our first place together, but instead of our own belongings, with mostly donated items our incredible friends and family helped band together in a couple week's time. That same year we got engaged and moved from Detroit to Chicago. Talk about an overwhelming, emotional roller coaster of a year filled with the polarizing highs and lows of loss and love.

Age 27, a few months after getting married and just a couple years after rebuilding a life of physical possessions, my husband and I turned around and sold nearly everything we owned and moved to Costa Rica. We had never been there before and I did not speak a lick of Spanish at the time. Exhilarating, albeit...overwhelming.

A little over two months after landing in Costa Rica with our dog and six suitcases, right when we began to get our bearings about us in a whole new life, my uncle Ricky, may he fly high in peace and love, took his own life in his basement. It was an entirely new experience of loss, both in circumstance and in being the farthest I had ever been from family. When someone you love is in enough pain to bring an end to their own existence on this planet you develop an entirely new perspective on just how fragile we each are.

And to close the decade, my truly *roaring* twenties, at age 29 my parents arrived in Costa Rica for a Christmas visit my Mom would never return home from. They arrived on December 23 and she thought she had a case of lingering pneumonia. On December 27 a doctor at a clinic in Costa Rica identified a tumor that had engulfed her entire left lung. On January 17 she was officially diagnosed with stage 4 lung cancer in the ICU at Hospital CIMA in San Jose, Costa Rica. And on February 11, she made her eternal voyage, holding hands with both my Dad and I, in the guest bedroom of the house my husband and I were renting. Just a few minutes after one final Morphine shot; our attempts had reached a mute point, failing to curb the unbearable, torturous pain at all.

I've learned *that's* the ultimate paradox in this life: not wanting to let someone go, but knowing it's best. Knowing their experience here will only get more painful with each second they stay. It was earlier that very same day I had finally reached a point to tell my Mom: "You can go. If you're ready you can go. We don't want to live without you, but we're going to be okay." She was ready and I'll be forever grateful I worked up the courage to offer her the peace of mind I knew she was waiting for.

At the beginning of this series of unfortunate events, I absolutely felt like a victim. "Why me" was rampant in my inner dialogue. Sometimes it still creeps in, but overall, my perspective has shifted. From "why me" to "this is a part of who I am. This is part of my story." There's a spiritual proverb I saw years ago, and I don't even know who to attribute it to, but it has always stuck with me:

> *"Your path is more difficult because your calling is higher."*

It doesn't resonate with me because I think what I've been through somehow trumps the many awful things so many people experience. Quite the opposite, it has humbled me. We can do all of the things to try and control our personal outcomes: get an education, give back, do good, sacrifice, work hard. And yet, we still don't get to choose our calling. Sometimes the reason we have the experiences we do is that life needs to step in and force us to take the turns we may not be prepared to take ourselves. If we get lost, something will happen to put us back on the path meant for us. Now more than ever, as scary and vulnerable as it feels to share, I have felt my calling. To share. Because life has taught me a lot. And what's the point of keeping it all bottled up?

Over the last decade-plus, I have explored *hundreds* of means and modalities. Everything from traditional talk therapy and prescription anxiety/depression medication, to traditional ayahuasca ceremonies in the Costa Rican countryside. When my Mom passed away, and I hit restart on yet another journey of grief and healing, I decided to start keeping a journal of the things I had tried and how helpful (or not) they were to me. Things that I could go to; when sadness felt inescapable, the thought of being "productive" led to self-loathing and even less motivation, and the idea of simply getting out of bed felt like too much to bear.

I put together this compilation of 25 things that have helped me the most – as a 'normal' person who has experienced life and its curveballs. These tools have been the guideposts helping me figure out ways to navigate those curveballs, and come out feeling stronger on the other side. My deepest desire in sharing these ideas is that they might help you too. Because our world needs a little more open honesty, and a little more authentic sharing. And I'm starting to understand that my calling in our world is greater than my fear of being vulnerable.

Happy Pillz Don't Always Come In Capsules...

1. START PRACTICING DAILY MEDITATION.

Meditation has been part of the mainstream conversation for several years now, and for so long I found myself curious but hesitant. Though I had practiced yoga for many years and been in circles of people who discussed a meditation practice, I didn't really know what it meant or how to do it. When my Mom passed away in 2017, I finally buckled down and gave it a real shot. When you wake up every day and feel the weighted blanket of sadness that is mourning, it makes even the simplest of tasks difficult to tackle. I knew I needed something to make the days feel lighter.

I recorded this video not too long after I began practicing meditation. I had come to the realization most people are intimidated to give it a try because they're overcomplicating it. There is no right or wrong way to meditate. The goal is not to achieve some altered state of mind in which you hack your own brain and shut off all of your thoughts (at least not as a beginner!). It's about learning to observe your own thought patterns with a greater sense of awareness and identify patterns you can then work with.

Even if you feel like your mind is racing the whole time, there's something to be said for forcing yourself to take even 10 minutes to sit and do nothing but close your eyes and breathe, knowing that you're doing it for your wellbeing. It's about taking the time to give your heart the reassurance you're worth those 10 minutes, just for you, outcome irrelevant.

There are a lot of free or inexpensive resources available today if you need some inspiration or guidance. Everything from breathing and counting techniques to guided meditations focusing on different mantras and subjects. I personally have found the Calm app to be really helpful and easy to use. I generally love the daily featured guided meditations, and some days if the subject matter doesn't speak to me, I choose a different one from their expansive library. I started with the free version and then ended up upgrading, and I have found it well worth a few dollars a month. I also like to sometimes search guided meditations on YouTube. Some of my favorites are by Sahdguru and Deepak Chopra.

You may find that the guidance is distracting to you, in which case, perhaps white noise or nature sounds or acoustic music playing in the background would be better.

2. CREATE A MORNING ROUTINE TO START EACH DAY WELL.

P articularly in long periods of sadness or overwhelm, like some of the more intense portions of a grief journey, you need a reason to get up to make getting out of bed easier. I learned instead of allowing myself to sleep until the last possible second before getting up for my first obligation of the day, creating space in the mornings for consistency and peace helped to set a more positive tone for my days. It certainly doesn't prevent you from having a bad day - they will happen. But it does increase the likelihood of more good days, and that's a step in the right direction. Like a built-in fresh start every morning you can count on.

I believe like so many things in life, there's no one size fits all solution. My morning routine has evolved over time. When I first started doing this, it started as making sure that I woke up early enough to have a *full hour* before I had to start getting ready for my first obligation of the day. This gave me time to meditate, play with my dog, have a cup of coffee, and be slow instead of rushed. Enough time to make sure I was starting each day in a way that felt calm and made me smile.

Today my morning routine is much more in-depth. I started to hold this time so sacred I wanted more and more of it. It turned me into a bonafide morning person! These days I wake up at 5 a.m. I never thought it possible for me to wake up so early, but this morning routine became *so* important and fulfilling to me, I gradually trained myself to wake up earlier and earlier for the sole purpose of having more me-time before the day had a chance to sweep me away.

❖ ❖ ❖

My mornings these days look something like this:

5:00 am - Make a cup of Amla Green tea and light an incense stick. Nag Champa by the brand Satya is my favorite. Stretch. Breathe.

5:30 am - Read for about an hour. (This is not "required" reading, although sometimes I'm choosing to read about business or personal development. The active choice is important.)

6:30 am - Make a cup of warm lemon water using the juice of an entire lemon, a little pink Himalayan salt and a dash of cayenne.

6:40 am - Meditate and pull a card from my favorite oracle card deck, because I'm into that sort of thing ;-)

7:00 am - Check email and organize my daily to-do list before the rest of the world starts buzzing. I thrive when my thoughts are organized. Do a little journaling if I skip email or if I have extra time.

7:35 am - Get dressed and pack gym bag

8:00 am - Hit the gym.

9:30 am - Hello world. I am available now :)

Maybe you don't have this much time. Maybe you have no desire to wake up that early. Maybe what would feel nourishing and satisfying to you looks completely different; but hopefully some ideas are flowing!

Some days I read less, meditate more. Some days my body is exhausted and I sleep an extra hour. The point of this is not to create more obligation for yourself, but rather create nourishing habits to *look forward* to.

Experiment with this. What will set your day off on the

right foot?

3. CREATE A CALMING BEDTIME RITUAL.

Bookends come in pairs! Bookend your day with space and time that feels safe, loving and peaceful. As the term "ritual" suggests – simplicity is key, because this is something you want to be able to do the same way over and over again. What you're doing is training your body and mind to wind down and be ready to welcome rest. Discover something easy to maintain, that doesn't require a lot of thought and that actually calms you.

Sleep is so important to our health in general, but particularly if we're experiencing a challenge or emotional upheaval. Sleep can be the difference between getting at least one important thing done in a day and getting absolutely nothing done and wallowing instead. This isn't groundbreaking, but worth reiterating: exhaustion doesn't do much to help with anxiety or overwhelm.

Lavender

I've known about the calming effects of lavender since I was a kid. It was my Mom's favorite flower and scent – she grew it in our garden, dried it, kept it in our house and kept lavender sprays in the house for everything from air freshener to pillow sprays. Incorporating lavender in some way was a no brainer. I diffuse lavender essential oil or burn a lavender incense at night before bed – you could also have a lavender plant in your room, keep it by your bedside in dried form or give your pillow a spritz – whatever floats your boat.

Aside from my personal, sentimental connection to lavender, it has been touted by experts for years as a natural supplement for sleep aid. Notably, it interacts with the neurotransmitter GABA to help quiet the brain and nervous system activity, which can have a great impact on reducing restlessness and anxious thoughts and feelings.

Tea

I also started drinking organic sleepy time tea before bed. I don't prefer a particular brand, but I do specifically look for teas with valerian root in them.

Similar to lavender, valerian root has been shown to have beneficial interactions with the GABA to promote relaxation. Valerian root is also known to contain antioxidants known for their sleep-enhancing properties. Consuming valerian in tea form is not likely to cause you any issue, but of course, here comes the "I am not a medical professional" disclaimer: if you decide to look into valerian in supplement form - be sure to discuss with your doctor, particularly if you take any medications - as with any supplement, you want to be careful of adverse interactions.

Having a soothing, warm cup of tea in one of my favorite mugs has become a cue to my body that we're winding down.

Quiet Your Mind

Avoid using your phone at night. The blue light emitted from the screen is a well-documented sleep disruptor at this point. Beyond that, scrolling social media or checking email right before bed does absolutely nothing to quiet the mind. Work has no place in the bedroom. Neither do other people's lives.

For me, I actually do my best to put my phone down for the last time about two hours before going to bed. And I leave my phone in the kitchen on the charger at night, I don't even take it in the bedroom with me anymore.

Banning my phone from the bedroom helped me accomplish two things. First, it eliminates the temptation to look at my phone. If a notification does come in, with the phone next to my bed it would be nearly impossible not to check. Out of sight out of mind; it works. It also prevents me from doing things like checking if my alarm is set 20 bajillion times, or mindlessly scrolling social media if I *am* restless and having a hard time drifting off. Second, enforcing this habit helped me to kick my former snooze habit to the curb. With the phone next to my bed, snooze always felt like "oh, it's just a few extra minutes." With my phone in the kitchen, there's no way to shut off the alarm other than to get my butt out of bed and walk out there - by that time, I'm up.

If my mind is particularly active I will try to read a few pages of a book. Not for the purpose of reading until I can't stay awake anymore, but to quiet my other thoughts and slow down my mind.

I mentioned the Calm app in the meditation section. They also have a feature called sleep stories, and as silly as it sounds – you know, bedtime stories for adults – I have found them refreshingly effective. They're typically read by narrators with very calming, subtle voices and tones, and the stories have very few crucial details so you're able to avoid feeling like you're straining to listen and pay attention. If my mind is running a million miles a minute and I can't turn it off, I turn one of those stories on and I'm usually asleep within minutes. If the suggestion to remove your phone from the bedroom resonates with you, but this does too, having your phone connected to a bluetooth speaker in the bedroom could give you the best of both options.

These are all of course things that have worked for me – for you it might be as simple as a warm shower before bed and turning on acoustic music lightly in the background. What you choose to do doesn't matter, so long as you find something that helps wash away the stress and overwhelm of the day before sleep.

Getting a good night's sleep works wonders when a bunch of other things start going awry in life.

4. IDENTIFY YOUR "HAPPY PILLS" AND HAVE THEM EASILY ACCESSIBLE.

I was flipping through a book about how to create a "dot journal" and while the overall process of creating a dot journal felt complicated and...overwhelming (ha!)...one of the suggestions was to dedicate a page to your "happy pills," and it stood out to me. So much so, it inspired the name for this book. Essentially a list of things you can use as a go-to if you're feeling down or in a funk, you know usually improve your mood.

These could be anything – some quick, others that require taking a break from your day – having a list to pick and choose from in moments you don't feel able to come up with creative solutions can be such a relief.

I'd imagine yoga or meditation would make their way onto a list like this for many people, given the calming, self-love focused nature of the two activities.

You could instantly feel your mood lift by listening to a particular song or artist; a perfect addition to your list.

Maybe you have a favorite drink or snack that always puts a smile on your face.

I am a total Ellen Degeneres fangirl and there are not many things guaranteed to make me laugh even in my darkest moments like Ellen. I find her hilarious and have always really enjoyed watching her interviews and show segments. I follow her on Instagram and if I need to put a smile on my face and do a quick reset, I know watching an Ellen clip or two will do just the trick. I feel the same way about Kevin Hart. They're both on my list.

Figure out what your happy pills are, and write them down in a place that's easily accessible to you whether it's in your day planner or on your phone – or maybe an actual dot journal is up your alley and you have a page there, as prescribed.

5. LEARN ABOUT THE TRANSFORMATIONAL BREATHING TECHNIQUE AND PRACTICE IT.

I know you may be thinking, what kind of foo foo, woo woo idea is this, and trust me I get it because when I first heard of it I thought along those same lines.

I was introduced to transformational breathwork through one of my now very dearest friends who is a facilitator, and I'm not exaggerating when I say it shifted my entire perspective and has changed my life.

It's a very simple, but specific method of breathing that allows you to target emotional blockages in the body and get them moving. It works wonders particularly if you're at a point in your life where you feel like you're lacking clarity or resolve – basically the definition of overwhelm. Am I right?

What I experience during a transformational breath session is almost always what I describe as an intense emotional release (I usually cry, **A LOT**). I've also had very visual experiences.

The tattoo I have on my forearm was a vision that came to me clear as day during a breath session. And this is not a drug people, this is your *own breath*. Sounds wild; you've just got to try it for yourself. I literally feel lighter coming out of these sessions.

There is a YouTube channel with some great introductory content and mini guided sessions to teach you about this method and how to start practicing it on your own – it's a great, FREE resource to get your feet wet and see what it's all about. A silver lining to come out of COVID (yes, there are silver lining's!) - she now offers virtual sessions you can book through her website as well.

Facilitators who lead guided transformational breath sessions also span the globe, so if you wanted to pay for an in-person session and really get a taste of the full experience you can check this website to see if there's someone available in your area.

When I opened myself to trying this method, I was amazed to learn what kind of energy I can shift and how I can alter my state of mind, simply through the power of my own breath – the most basic yet crucial of bodily functions.

6. WRITE YOURSELF A LETTER ON A GOOD DAY.

In 2018 my husband and I unexpectedly learned we would have to move back to the United States from Costa Rica due to a technicality in immigration law (my husband is a US Green Card holder, not a US citizen).

We were about to break ground on our dream home in Costa Rica. The plans were done, the plot had been cleared, the builder was ready and we were about to pull permits from the local municipality. At the table having lunch, I cried my eyes out telling our builder, and friend, we couldn't move forward with the project. I'll never forget him hugging us and telling us "The plans will be here. If this is meant to be it'll be. Life needs you to go in a different direction for a while, that's all. You're gonna find out why."

So to save my husband's legal status in the United States, we pulled the plug on the project and headed back to be in the United States full time again. We were left with the decision to move anywhere we wanted in the United States. Sounds like an exciting prospect in theory, but in reality it was quite, you may have guessed…overwhelming.

My mind was reeling for weeks after our stark new reality began to set in and despite my best efforts, I was angry. Sad. Devastated, really. I didn't want to leave Costa Rica and nothing felt right. Then a suggestion from a therapist caught my attention, a 'snap out of it' moment: write yourself a letter on a good day.

As you begin to process bad news, or unexpected news – there will be highs and lows as with any natural life cycle. For all the shitty days, there *will* be days where the innate feeling that primes us all for survival pokes through: the one you feel in your heart saying "yeah, everything's gonna be alright."

Her suggestion was, on one of those days, when you catch yourself feeling good and optimistic, write yourself a letter and tell yourself all the things you know to be true. Write about all the things you'd like to give yourself permission to look forward to as an outcome or result of whatever transition period you're currently in.

I took this advice and wrote myself a letter one day - and have done this exercise several times since. But here is the first one I wrote to myself, just before planning our first trip to St. Petersburg, FL to start our *new* house hunting journey:

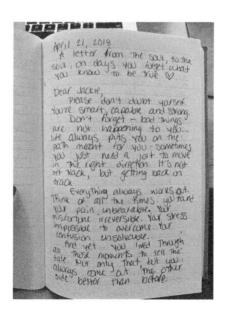

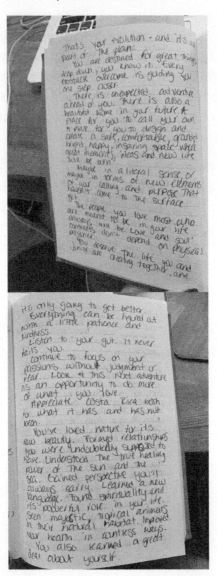

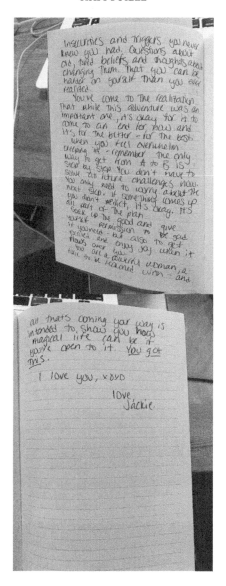

I wrote about surviving past hardships, and all the good things I imagined could come from this unexpected news. And as we continued to move through the process of planning our move, and figuring out all of the many logistics, on days where I felt overwhelm start to bubble over... I read my letter. I was amazed by the way positive reinforcement, love and advice *from myself* shifted the entire dynamic of what I was feeling and provided me instant relief.

I told a friend about this and she said "Yeah that's a good idea! It's like kicking your own ass to remember that everything is gonna work out!" It made me laugh because the way she said it was funny, but also because it's so incredibly simple and yet deeply true. Sometimes, you need to kick your own ass.

7. DRINK MORE WATER.

T his might sound silly, but doing basic things like drinking enough water are often the things we neglect when we're getting caught up in the torment of our own minds.

When we're overwhelmed, sad, anxious, depressed - one of the most common symptoms or side effects is feeling sluggish and lacking motivation. You can go ahead and triple or quadruple that effect if you allow yourself to become dehydrated. It makes your skin dry and uncomfortable, causes headaches and fatigue, causes cramping, inhibits your ability to focus or sleep and the list goes on.

Do whatever you need to do to drink more water, even *more* than you normally would! Buy yourself a cute, oversized water bottle. A HydroFlask or Yeti or the like, something that keeps your water extra cold and refreshing and incentivizes you to drink it is always worth a splurge – much more so probably than whatever else you might be thinking of buying if you're a retail therapy type. *Hint Hint:* Buy things that will have a positive impact on your actions and habits.

Soak fruit in your water or squeeze a lemon into it if you need it to taste like something. Intermittently drink some soda water if a little fizz makes it more interesting for you.

Eating more fruits with a high water content, like watermelon, pineapple, citrus fruits or grapes can also help increase your state of hydration and help you do it without feeling like you're constantly filling your belly with water.

For a super boost, incorporate drinking coconut water. It has a light, refreshing taste – not everyone loves it, but it's worth a shot. It's 100% natural so you avoid negatives like added sugar but get a huge concentration of electrolytes in as little as one cup. Coconut water is rich in nutrients including vitamin C, magnesium (which studies have shown a large portion of the population in the US happens to be deficient in), manganese, potassium and calcium.

Don't underestimate the **basics** when it comes to maintaining your overall physical health in your efforts to also take care of your emotional health when the going gets tough.

8. EAT GOOD FOOD –
WHEN YOU EAT LIKE CRAP,
YOU FEEL LIKE SHIT.

When you physically feel like shit, what do you think it does to your mindset? This is another one that may feel really obvious but can be incredibly difficult to commit to when you're down and out. When you're feeling down in the dumps and fed up with life it can be undeniably easy to reach for chips and salsa or the frozen pizza instead of preparing and eating a good meal. Do anything and everything you have to do to make eating well a priority. If you have the means to subscribe to a meal service or hire someone to help you shop, do it. If you need to trade a friend something you can help them with for some accountability, do that.

The easiest way to stick to this? Don't have the crap in your house. If chips and salsa are a go-to, write "veggies and hummus" on your hand before you go to the grocery store. Write out a list of all your guilty pleasures, and then write "=" followed by a healthier alternative for each. When you're wandering the aisles you have a support plan to help you make better choices than a knee jerk, emotional reaction to the plethora of options before you. Take some time to invest in planning your nutrition a little bit and if you make nothing else a priority, vow to yourself and your health that this will stay at the top of the list no matter what.

Yes, this may all be difficult, but I can promise you: making strides toward a healthier physical existence is 100% easier than working through healing emotional traumas and exercising your mind to support you through the overwhelm of life. The heart work is the hard work. So start with the low hanging fruit. If you feel like you're fighting an uphill battle, making better food choices is actually at the bottom of the totem pole in terms of actionable, tangible steps in a better direction. This doesn't mean trying to accomplish an entire diet and lifestyle overhaul over-night. But it does mean biting the bullet and taking baby steps.

I find visual reminders to be very helpful. I honestly can't remember where I stumbled across these particular affirmations that have been so helpful to me, but wher-ever I heard or saw them, I'm grateful. Reminders that help you may be different, but I chose to write these on a postcard and look at them every single day on the front of my fridge.

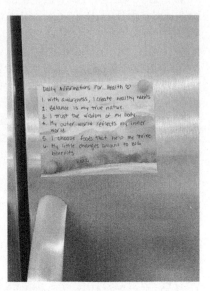

We so often look at our mind and body as two separate entities to care for, but I've learned so much from adapt-ing more of a 360-degree approach and seeing the way one interacts with the other.

There's no magic button to make this one easier, but it's es-sential and makes a monumental difference. While there's access to a wide array of tips and tricks and information on this topic in our digital world, some general guidelines that have really helped me on my journey are these:

- Focus on eating as many whole foods as possible, in their original form. Yes. This means lots of fruits, veggies, potatoes, legumes, beans, rice. Things you can buy *without* a label. Or if there is a label, the one and ONLY ingredient is the food item itself.

- Avoid processed foods (anything in a package) and if/when you must buy processed foods, look for things with four ingredients or less. Can you find options? How close can you get to this minimal in-gredient guideline? This is always an eye-opening exercise in the grocery store and will start to have you evaluate food choices differently. The good ol' "if there's an ingredient you don't recognize or can't pronounce, best to steer clear" guideline is also simple to put into practice.

- Experiment with jazzing food up with spices and seasonings instead of dressings or sauces.

- And as mentioned previously, simply don't buy junk food (or what I call "trigger food" - food you turn to on auto-pilot when you're in one of those 'eat your feelings' moods). Save these things for a treat you might eat at a restaurant or social gather-ing.

No matter how much you "don't feel like it," this is one of those things where you just have to kick yourself in the ass (here we go with that again) and DO IT. Trust me, I get it. There was a time, during those roaring twenties when I ate carryout for every single meal, every single day. And paid Starbucks about $500 a month to boot. I've been in that place of knowing I was making the worst possible choices but doing it anyway in the name of temporary satisfaction, convenience, ease and minimal effort. Today, I'm at a place in my life where the foods I put in my body are almost al-ways the best quality for nourishment and optimal health. It took me about six years of conscious effort to get to the place I'm in now - where I feel extremely confident and really damn good about my new go-to food choices in life. It's not a snap of your fingers, but you have to start somewhere.

A major key here is simply taking the action of preparing more of your own food vs. eating out. Being able to avoid the butters and oils restaurant foods are so often drenched in during prep is already a huge leap forward in supporting yourself nutritionally! One thing that made it *a lot* easier for me to get into the groove of making my own food was investing in kitchen gadgets like the InstantPot (which doubles as a pressure cooker and slow cooker) and an air fryer. The internet is littered with minimal prep, mostly hands-off recipes specifically for use with these sweet do-dads. For example, I can type "lentil soup in the instant pot", and I'd get an ingredient list and 'chop everything up, throw it in, and walk away until it's done' instructions. Another thing I love about these tools is they allow you to cook in larger batches so that in one prep session, you make enough food for multiple meals. **Your small changes will amount to big benefits.**

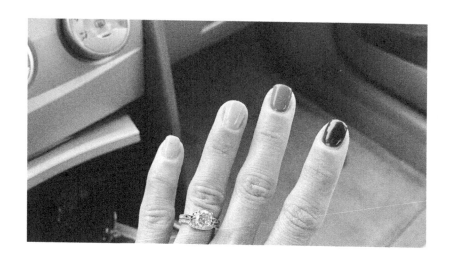

9. PRIORITIZE PERSONAL
GROOMING RITUALS THAT
MAKE YOU FEEL GOOD.

B efore you roll your eyes thinking "is this chick really reminding me to shower regularly and wear deodorant?" rest assured...I'm not. Although, those daily action items may also help you feel your best.

What I'm saying is prioritize some of the extra stuff that you know makes you feel good in your own skin. For guys, it could be a professional beard trim – or going to one of those parlors where they offer a neck massage with your hair cut – it might be a few dollars more, but if you walk out feeling like a million bucks, isn't it worth it?

I'm talking about the bubble baths, the face masks, the eyebrow threading vs. trying to pluck on your own...Whatever *it* is... I think we all have that one thing we absolutely love, but we often end up categorizing it as a guilty pleasure or luxury. Why? Life is busy so we push our self-care to the bottom of our list of priorities, when really, especially if we're going through a tough time, those things should be at the very top.

For me, it's getting my nails done. Nothing gives me an extra pep in my step than a fresh mani/pedi. It boosts my confidence and gives me an edge. Even if I'm down in the dumps, I know going to get my nails done will cheer me up.

This doesn't have to be expensive or a big to-do. I mentioned a few examples, but there are loads of things you can do at home, for little or no money that require very little effort or time. Flea markets, farmer's markets and local open-air fairs are great places to find local, mom-and-pop apothecary-style businesses that make health and beauty products. This can be a fun way to try something new in the way of facial or body products you can infuse into your routine. The bonus is that these small, local vendors are often making products using natural, more ethically sourced ingredients than anything you can buy at the store; so you get the benefit of supporting a local business and a better-for-you product too! Make the time, ditch the guilt, and do what you have to do to feel good in your body – you owe it to yourself and no one needs an explanation from you.

10. WORKOUT.

"**A**nother obvious one?! What did I even buy this book for??" If this suggestion makes you feel defensive, you need to hear it. If your mind is taking you for a ride and you can't seem to get out of a funk, moving your body IS GOING TO HELP! We need to tend to the physical in order to support the mental.

Amidst a world of conflicting science and blurry lines of merit, there's *zero* debate about the fact that physical activity produces endorphins in the brain, which are a group of hormones best known for their ability to reduce feelings of both physical and emotional pain and can induce feelings of euphoria or pleasure.

I know plenty of people who would say:
 "Working out isn't easy for everyone," or
 "It's not exactly 'enjoyable' to sweat and exert yourself," or
 "I don't know where to start," or the classic
 "I don't have time/motivation."
 The *excuses* (or defense mechanisms) are limitless.

Working myself into a routine with daily physical activity has saved me from myself more times than I can count. When you're emotionally exhausted, even 20 minutes of exercise can mean the difference between beating yourself up for doing absolutely nothing that day and having made the effort to at least do *something*. An important distinction when you're trying to build yourself up. Getting moving often leads toward the shifting of emotions and clears space for that elusive "motivation" to do other things too...

When I tell you to workout, I'm simply saying start somewhere. Incorporate some kind of physical activity into your day that normally wouldn't be there. This could be vowing to take the stairs instead of the elevator. Taking the dog for a walk around the block instead of letting him out in the backyard before work. Walking a couple of laps around the parking lot at work during lunch. Everything from the simple all the way up to the bigger choices like joining a gym, signing up for classes or practicing yoga.

I've always been a pretty physically active person and I have to say I always had a little skepticism about how much better working out can *actually* make you feel mentally. I've always done it because I wanted to and it's just always been a part of my life. But honestly I never really knew what benefits could be attributed to working out in times I was feeling down or whether those benefits were coming from another source.

Over the past couple of years though, I've had a couple of points that truly felt like rock bottom, and I decided to pay closer attention.

Though working out is sometimes the absolute last thing I want to do when I'm feeling particularly sorry for myself, once I started observing my own patterns, I inevitably noticed *always* feeling better after getting a workout in. It's the starting that's most difficult, but once you get moving, you're golden.

When you're overwhelmed, "not feeling like doing anything" is one of the physical manifestations of that level of mental fatigue. It applies to working out and virtually anything else that requires thought or effort. How do you push past that?

Mel Robbins' 5-second rule changed my life. You can find several different talks of hers on YouTube and I highly recommend watching. The synopsis that's relevant here is when you don't *feel like* doing something, you have 5 seconds to either take action or talk yourself out of it. Whether you're going to try and wake up an hour earlier and workout in the morning or if you're going to fit it in during lunch, after work or on the weekend, there's going to be that moment before you have to get up and get ready to go do whatever it is you're going to do. You're likely not going to feel like it, because that's the trend with this overwhelm stuff...everything feels like a real chore, and chores generally don't sound like a ton of fun.

Mel Robbins would say, at *that* moment you have 5 seconds to get your butt in gear and get going. You literally need to count down in your head (or out loud), "5-4-3-2-1," and by the time you get to 1, you know you have to have your feet on the floor, getting out of bed or out of your chair and off of Facebook. Wherever the point of resistance is, that's where you insert your countdown. Out loud. 5-4-3-2-1.

Putting the countdown into practice is simple and it's an easy way to hold yourself accountable to do things even when you don't feel like it. If you're feeling pretty crumby all around, the chances of you waking up one morning and being truly chipper to go and workout are slim. You've gotta take matters into your own hands and figure it out. 5-4-3-2-1-GO.

11. ACTIVELY IDENTIFY ONE THING YOU'RE GRATEFUL FOR EVERY SINGLE DAY.

Y ou've probably heard of the concept of a gratitude journal, and this is a simplified version. It's really amazing to observe the difference it makes – mind, body and spirit – when you make a shift toward focusing on what you have to be grateful for. I like the practice of identifying just one thing because even on the most awful of days, if you're alive, you have at least one thing to be grateful for.

In order for this to become helpful to you, you need to be consistent. It can't just be thinking about things in your head, or saying in conversation "I know I have a lot to be grateful for, but..." No. Strike the "but." That is you starting with gratitude and ending with lethargy and a return to the negative. It defeats the purpose.

Choose a place you're going to write down, or verbalize the one thing you're grateful for every day. This could be recording voice memos for yourself or writing it down in your day planner, a journal or notebook. You could even choose a buddy – someone you think could also benefit from the practice – and text them each day.

The point here is fairly obvious. If you haven't noticed a trend already, out of the hundreds of things I have tried over the years, some of the simplest have been the most beneficial, with practice and consistency. Even when we're really down in the dumps and don't know what to do or where to turn – there is *something* to be grateful for. It could be something big, like the love of a spouse, family member or dear friend – or it could be something simple and in the moment like waking up and hearing the cheerful sound of birds chirping, or that it's sunny out and you will have a chance to go for a walk.

After spending a consistent period of time doing this daily, you will notice even if your current dilemma or stress or sadness has not resolved, you're finding it easier to come up with one thing per day you genuinely feel grateful for – and *that*, is the shift you're looking for. You may have heard the expression "where your attention goes, energy flows" and that's exactly the point of intentionally focusing on gratitude each day.

Dedicating yourself to giving this practice a genuine shot will go to work for you in your subconscious on a daily basis to continually raise your energetic frequencies and help put you in a better headspace to tackle the tough stuff.

12. SET AN INTENTION DAILY.

I'm not talking about to-do list stuff. When you're feeling overwhelmed it's no wonder the societal habit of hyper-focusing on everything you have to do provides no relief whatsoever. The daily intention however is more of a broad stroke. How do you want to show up for the day? What's the tone you'd set in an ideal world? Maybe you're not going to move the mountain today, but what would help you tighten the laces on your climbing shoes?

Setting a daily intention can even be something that you do in combination with #11 – in the same spot or with the same buddy.

When I say set an intention, I want your mind to go to the realm of self-love, emotional health and well-being and creating space for the way you want each day to *feel* and play out. I've set daily intentions as simple as "my intention for the day is to welcome calm and peace." I've also had days where I choose to be pretty specific based on what I'm going through. Something like "my intention today is to pause before reacting to comments people think are comforting and remember they are simply doing their best to connect."

> *One of my favorite daily intentions, that I use on a regular basis because I notice what a difference it makes in my day is: "my intention for the day is to actively notice all the things and moments that make me smile." Actively and consciously setting out to notice smiles throughout the day has been such a beautiful reminder that there are indeed smiles in each and every day. Sometimes we just allow them to be overshadowed by our preoccupation with all the noise and all the stuff that's not going our way.*

About 3 years ago, I joined a Whatsapp group with four girlfriends that we still maintain today. It was started by my friend who also happens to be a spiritual coach, author and speaker, Paola Castro. I'll leave her website here as a bonus resource for you ;-) I'm certain at some point she will share something that will get you thinking, bring you a smile, or help you breathe through a difficult moment - because that's the kind of human she is.

We've gone through long streaks of high consistency in this group, and sometimes some of us drop off for a while and then come back. Through some of my darkest times, this simple message group has been my silver lining. The power of accountability, and sharing your gratitudes and intentions *with others* is truly special. That's precisely why I make the suggestion of finding a buddy for so many of the tools and tips I recommend.

While you and your buddy could choose any format that feels easy and natural, in our group, each day, we each share:
1. One thing we're grateful for.
2. Our intention for the day.
3. One task to complete that day (we say, the one thing that if you got it done, the day would feel like a success).
4. 'Yes' or 'no' to: "did you complete yesterday's task?" *There's that accountability ;-)*

Sometimes little side conversations spark. Sometimes we inspire each other with our gratitude's and intentions and give each other ideas for where we could place our focus. Sometimes we each simply share our four and that's the end of it. But we know we put it out into the world. And it's powerful.

13. MAKE A LIST OF FEELINGS/ EMOTIONS YOU WANT TO FEEL.

Make a list of feelings and emotions you want more of in your life and keep them in an easily accessible place.

Here's an example from my own journal:

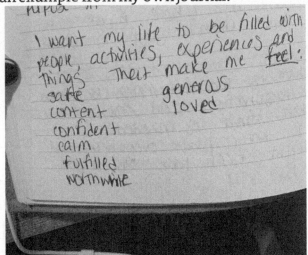

Give yourself a challenge time period. Long enough to gather enough data let's call it, but also a time period you feel you can actually achieve. Maybe 15 or 30 days? Keep a tiny journal, notepad, sticky notes or the like (something easy to carry around with you). Every time you do or experience something that elicits one of the feelings or emotions you included on your list, write it down.

Sometimes when we feel stuck in a particularly long rut of overwhelm, we feel lost. As if we don't even know what we want anymore or *what* makes us happy. What you've done for yourself with this exercise is create a glossary of things and activities that make you feel the way you want to feel.

It's easy for us to lose sight of these things simply because we get too overwhelmed to slow down a little and pay attention. I've found this exercise can be really helpful to reign yourself in, get grounded and remember (or discover) what makes you feel good. What makes you feel like YOU.

14. CRY. ALLOW YOURSELF TO HAVE THE BAD DAYS.

T oo often we're inundated with messages that hype up optimism and positivity and smiling and sunshine. Not that any of those things are bad. Not by a long shot. Not that we don't all want and NEED those elements in our life. But to think we can sustain butterflies and rainbows all the time is just plain out of touch. Worthy of note as well, the positive emotions are not the only ones important to our being human. Sometimes you just feel like "Fuck. This. Shit." And that's human! That's real! That's OKAY!

Particularly in Western culture, we are conditioned from a young age that crying is a sign of weakness. That the goal when crying is to stop crying as quickly as possible. That other people are allowed to judge what is worthy of our tears. Ever hear an adult say to a child "that's no reason to cry," or give a kid a countdown to *stop* crying before they'll continue talking? Or go to break up with your high school boyfriend or girlfriend and preempt your bad news by saying "please don't cry, but..." Or been told the boardroom is no place for tears and that it's "business, not personal?"

No wonder crying gets a bad rap; it's ingrained in us.

Our bodies cry because it's a necessary bodily function and expression of human emotion. Hear me when I type: The. Human. Body. Would. Not. Cry. If. It. Were. Not. Meant. To.

Don't be bullied by childhood narratives, outdated notions or Instagram memes into thinking you're having a pity party or being "negative" by allowing yourself to have a bad day. We can learn just as much by letting ourselves cry as we can from sucking it up and powering through.

There's space in life to do both, and both are highly necessary.

This one is simple. Cry sometimes and don't feel one bit bad about it.

Ever have a moment with your internal dialogue? "I'm not going to cry over this, breathe, I'm not going to do it." That would be a perfect time to tell yourself to 'shut up' and let the waterworks flow. ;-)

If you're feeling filled with sadness, rage, frustration, confusion...stop and ask yourself to recall when the last time you had a good cry was. If you can't remember or it's been a while, refer back to #5 and try a breath session. See if you can get those emotions MOVING. All emotions are meant to be temporary. They are meant to flow through us, not to be held in. Similar to the line on a heart monitor, the fluctuations are what mean we're alive. The flat line indicates stagnancy. No future change is equivalent to death.

Embrace your emotion so that when it comes time to pass, you have no unfinished business with it and you'll feel the power and relief for yourself. The purpose of the low points is the rebound. In order to hit the highs, you have to go down low first.

15. AVOID UNNECESSARY OBLIGATIONS. JUST SAY NO.

Despite what life as we know it might make you think, we do not have limitless energy to go-go-go all the time. And just because we have a job and friends and family does not mean we're obligated to give every waking second of our time to those entities, despite the pressure we may feel, real or imagined. In the best of times certain expenditures of your energy are finite, let alone when you're having a rough go. Using that energy up on unnecessary things you feel "obligated" to is detrimental to both your physical and emotional health.

Many times when we deal with symptoms like fatigue, or general lack of interest in activity or socialization, it's because we've got an energy leak and we need to plug the holes.

The best, and probably most relatable example I can think of for this is parties where you feel forced to buy things. You know the ones I'm talking about. People host parties for everything from jewelry and cookware and essential oils to purses and sex toys. And we inevitably feel obligated to go to them because the person hosting is a friend or has been to an event that we've hosted before. And now, a lot of these events have become virtual. Piling on an extra layer of guilt, "It's so easy, you don't even have to leave your house!" But the real, actual truth is, we have no obligation to do anything we don't have the energy for. No matter who's hosting. Period.

The same goes for reunions. Girl's nights. Guy's nights. Happy hours. Wedding and baby showers. Uh oh. Things are getting squirmy now. "I can skip out on those things?" Yes. Yes you can. The RSVP card comes with a 'no' option for a *reason*. You can send a gift to be cordial.

People planning events *know* (or at least anyone with a smidge of emotional intelligence) not everyone will be able to make it. If it doesn't work for YOU, you just can't swing it, and that's perfectly acceptable. Remember, the people you want in your life are the ones who understand this anyway.

It's time to put an end to the stigma that evaluating our own energy before deciding to do something with or for others is selfish. You've heard it a thousand times: "you can't pour from an empty cup," and yes, that actually means something.

Believe it or not, your friend is not going to stop being your friend because you didn't show up to [name the thing]. If they do, they weren't that great of a friend to begin with. And this goes for *anything* you're invited to do. It's an *invitation*, not an obligation.

in-vi-ta-tion
/ˌinvəˈtāSH(ə)n/
noun
a written or verbal request inviting someone to go somewhere or to do something.

Key word: *request*.

While we're shedding unnecessary obligations, it doesn't hurt to shed people who don't really care about our best interests either. You will feel more lonely around 100 people who are not an energetic match for you, than you will with one really great friend, or even better yet, a headspace that allows you to genuinely enjoy your own company.

This one is a lot easier said than done, but my favorite

piece of advice here is to just let things like this work themselves out naturally. Give it a try. Go with exactly how you feel. Decline as many invitations as you want. Say 'no' to as much as you want. When you stop agreeing to do things you don't actually want to do, with people you don't actually want to do them with, these things tend to naturally ebb and flow. It doesn't have to be a dramatic "I don't want you in my life anymore."

At a certain point, it's also time to understand, our friendships and the activities associated with them will start to silo themselves. You'll have different levels and different categories of friendship and social relationships and each come with their own set of boundaries. Don't be afraid of this. Embrace it. Some friendships will be the kind you want to call and tell each other everything and go on vacation together for a week and it'll still feel too short. Others, you will only ever do particular activities together; maybe related to where you met or how you know one another. Some you'll see a couple times a year and you'll each understand life is busy, and come to cherish the time you *do* get to spend together without expecting more.

Here are some question formats to run through, if you're feeling anxious about obligation vs. choice:
"If I don't do X, will I lose Y?"
"Is this required for my partner to feel supported or for success in our relationship?"
"Is it dangerous to my health or safety if I say no?"
"Is this required to properly, adequately care for my child or animal?"
"Is this something I explicitly gave my word on? And if so, what does the integrity of my word mean to ME in this

scenario?"

These basic questions can really help you narrow down true obligations; other than instances where the answers to these questions confirm required action, you don't owe anything to anyone.

Get used to the idea that the risk of temporarily bumming someone out is worth it to preserve your own energy, particularly at a time you really need it. And they will understand, probably more than you may think. It's hard to say "no," but the more you practice, not only does it get easier, but you realize how beneficial it is to be just as comfortable saying 'no' to things as you are saying 'yes'.

Protecting your energy is one of the most selfless things you can do for yourself. Read that again. Yes, selflessness can also point inward; there's a person in there in need of your unconditional love and support.

16. BUY A JOURNAL.

Whether you consider yourself a "writer" or not, there is something highly therapeutic about getting thoughts and ideas out of your head – even if they go nowhere other than onto a piece of paper. I found journal prompts helped me make this a regular practice. And helped give me direction on days when I was so overwhelmed I didn't know what to do or where to turn. You can find them in a lot of places – many bloggers, yoga instructors, career coaches, life coaches, etc. will offer journal prompts on their websites, blog posts or social media. A simple Google search will likely return a lot of ideas to get you started.

Here are some journal prompts I have found, tweaked, used, and loved:

- A longer form one that can be used in full or in pieces is to write out the following when you sit down to journal:
  - 1 thing (or 10!) you're grateful for
  - 1 thing that worked well (yesterday or today)
  - 1 thing you could improve (about the day, or in general)
  - 3 things you want to accomplish (relatively short term)
  - 3 ways you can take better care of yourself
  - 3 steps you can take to get you closer to where you need to be (this can be a specific goal, an improved emotional headspace, a physical health goal, etc.)
  - 3 great topics or ideas (this should pertain to you and what makes you feel creative or excited. It could be ideas for writing, ideas for your work, ideas for things you want to improve around your home, things you want to

learn about, etc.)

- The 'letter on a good day' suggestion from #6 can double as a journal entry.
- So often feelings of overwhelm come from fear, and I have found journaling around fear specifically to be powerful. Here are some questions you can use as starting points:
  - In an idyllic day dream, your world is perfect in one year. Where are you and what are you doing assuming all obstacles have been removed?
  - If later on you understood you didn't accomplish those goals (from idyllic scenario in question 1) because you ran away, were too afraid to start or gave up, how would that make you feel?
  - What lies do you tell yourself about why you can't accomplish your biggest dreams and how do they show up in your life as insecurities?
  - What does it look like when you put off your goals and let fear lead the way? What are you doing instead of pursuing your goals?
  - No filter. What are your BIGGEST fears when thinking of putting action to your creative dreams?
  - If you were to take *some* action, what are some realistic steps you could take to protect yourself from your worst-case scenario fears? (*Ex. I could save up 3 months of salary so when I quit my day job to pursue my own business, I have a few months' security to figure it out.*)
  - Aside from your goals themselves, what other great things could come from recogniz-

ing your fear and pushing it aside? More confidence? Better quality relationships? Knowledge or experience?

If a formal journal exercise feels like too much, you can always go with the good ol' stopwatch, freewrite method. Set the timer for whatever feels good; 10, 15, 20 minutes. In that time, JUST WRITE. It doesn't have to make sense, be grammatically correct, be formed of sentences or paragraphs. It can be as neat or sloppy as your brain and hand will produce. The goal is simply to not allow your pencil or pen to stop. Write constantly for whatever time you've set, and write down literally whatever is coming to your mind in all its glorious randomness (or surprising coherence). This is a GREAT exercise in clearing mental space and energy, and oftentimes in getting out of your own way.

Another cathartic journal exercise I've found especially helpful when in a headspace of perpetual negative thoughts is what I like to call "burn it down." When I'm unable to turn off the negative swirl of my mind, I'll get out my journal and write down every negative thought I have in my head until I either a.) Run out of negative thoughts or b.) My hand is so exhausted I can't write anymore.

Then I tear the pages out, fold them up and kiss them. This probably sounds like a scene out of a teenage chick flick, but the meaning is deeper. We need to practice compassion for ourselves if we're going to move through and beyond our darkest days. This includes compassion for the negative thought patterns that sometimes captivate us. For me the kiss is symbolic of saying "thank you for serving your purpose, goodbye." Then I burn the pages. Do this in a coffee can or a fire pit or something; please don't burn your house down...just the journal pages will do ;-) Follow this exercise with some act of self love - as simple as a cup of your favorite tea or as boujee as going straight for a manicure. Whatever time will allow, whatever you can swing - something to remind you that YOU are **separate** from the negative thoughts you just purged.

17. TALK ABOUT THE FUTURE
YOU WANT OUT LOUD, AS
IF IT'S THE PRESENT.

As you already know from the story I shared in #6 about my husband's and my abrupt and initially unwanted return to the United States; while it turned out to be the perfect next step for us in life, we didn't know it at the time. At the time, on top of still grieving my Mother's tragic death in Costa Rica; we were also grieving the perfect home we designed and were about to build in the jungle overlooking the ocean, that would no longer be.

It was an overwhelming (at first, devastating) blow to our plans. We were put on an extremely limited timeline to figure out how to appropriately cancel our plans with our builder in Costa Rica, figure out where we were going to move and how we were going to get our animals there. There's about a million and one logistics that go into an international move. We were thrown into three months of grueling, seemingly endless rounds of obstacles and "figuring things out" which ultimately included the decision to buy a house in the States. I was at a point in my life where my Cancer, home-loving soul craved nothing more than a place truly of my own. I needed comfort and security more than ever.

But instead of being filled with HGTV-style house-hunting enthusiasm, I was full of fear. Because of the time constraints and circumstance, we were going to be buying a house in a city we knew next to nothing about. Having just come off of the high of being completely in love and enamoured by the house we designed and were planning to build, every other house we looked at felt like a disappointment. Not to mention our 3 most recent tax years worth of foreign-earned income exclusion tax returns made financing back in the States a real pain.

The process of visualizing (and journaling) and role playing about the outcome of all of this is what got me through. Whenever I had the chance or even a few minutes to myself, I spent time talking about (to myself, to my husband, to the dog, to my friends, to my journal – whoever, whatever!) the future as if the entire pain-staking process of making the move happen was already over. I talked about our new house and how comfortable and inspiring it was, well before we were anywhere near having found one. I'd randomly look over at my husband while we were making lunch or dinner and say things like "hey, our new house is the shit, I love it here!"

I talked about all the things I felt re-inspired and motivated to do in my new space and how nice it was to look out the window and see the sunshine, before I had any idea what it would actually look or feel like. I talked about how well we acclimated and how much we were loving our new adventure, before I had any idea that would actually come to LOVE St. Petersburg, FL.

Focusing on what *could be* got me through the frustration of what currently was. Sound familiar? A-la-law of attraction perhaps? Where your attention goes, energy flows, remember? If you're constantly talking about and focusing on how shitty things are right now, you're not calling in the energy to support how great things could eventually be. Treat yourself to suspended reality, talk about the way you'd like things to be as if they are the present moment and you'll be surprised by the shift you notice. Think back to drama class in high school and learning how to improv; you can do it.

I've been more grateful for our house every single day than

I've ever been for a physical *thing*. It came down to the wire, our house. We were outbid, about to reluctantly put in an offer on our second choice, and the morning of, our competing bidders lost their financing and we were able to go under contract with our top choice. We closed on the house 3 days after arriving back in the United States and my husband and I talk at least once a week about how we feel more at "home" in our house than either of us have felt anywhere in our entire lives.

There was so much conscious energy poured into creating this reality, I can't help but to smile and think "wow, that really worked."

18. SPLURGE ON LITTLE
THINGS TO BRIGHTEN
YOUR PHYSICAL SPACE.

I'm not a supporter of retail therapy. I believe buying physical things to drown out feelings and emotions in an attempt to "pick ourselves up" can be just as detrimental to our health as emotional eating, substance use/abuse, etc.

HOWEVER. I do believe our physical space and surroundings have a major impact on our mental and physical health, and there are certain categories where splurging may be appropriate and helpful to some extent. Getting ourselves out of a challenging time can be just as complicated as the circumstance that got us there in the first place - so it's a matter of trying lots of different things to see what works and what doesn't.

There's plenty of studies around our physical space and the way it affects our mental state. Keeping things organized vs. cluttered for example has been proven time and time again to improve focus. When you're overwhelmed and your mind is a mess, anything to potentially improve focus is worth a shot.

So: before you splurge, purge. Go through one room, one closet at a time. Get rid of clutter and things you don't need or use. Put together things to donate; you'll get a dose of endorphins by doing good for others and clear out your space at the same time.

Once you're at a place that feels clear from the unnecessary, put some thought into what things around your house put a smile on your face when you look at them or use them. For me it's adorning my home with decorative elements that are oftentimes also deeply sentimental. I have framed photos from travels, a little shrine of sorts dedicated to my Mom with a piece of blown glass that has some of her ashes inside and a few other decorative knick knacks that belonged to her and remind me of her instantly, a few family heirlooms displayed.

I also love art. I have eclectic style and like all different mediums. And I never shy away from paying for a piece of art I know will bring me joy every time I look at it.

If you're surrounded by blank walls, decor might be an example of something you look to invest a little money in.

Comfortable seating is another example. In this pandemic era especially - spending some money on creating a truly comfortable yet functional, inspiring, aesthetically pleasing space might be well worth it for both your personal and professional sanity.

◆ ◆ ◆

There are smaller things that can make a big difference too.

I'm the dog lover of all dog lovers. One year my mom bought me one of those daily flip calendars from Dog Shaming and I swear on even the worst days, it made me smile and giggle. I ended up keeping it for three years and cycling back through the dates even though the year was wrong, just because I enjoyed it so much. That's gotta be worth $10 or $15 right?

Your sensory experience within your space can also be a game changer. I bought warm "yellow light" Edison bulbs for the bedside lamps in my bedroom for example, and I swear the color of the light makes my room much more calming and soothing before bed when I'm reading or going through my nighttime routine. Himalayan salt lamps are another example of something that would provide ambient lighting (amongst other benefits).

On the sensory track, what your space smells like may be a mood lifter depending on your personality and preferences. Think about this: in a retail setting, there are entire teams of people dedicated to store design down to every last detail including how the store *smells*. Why? Because it lifts people's spirits and they spend more time, and buy more things when they're having a pleasant sensory experience. Same goes for hotels and how well you sleep in them. Why not apply these same principles to your home? Candles, incense, diffusers and essential oils...whatever your preference, splurge away on household items to please your senses!

Plants. While house plants can easily turn into a pricey endeavor, they're well worth the spending over something that would bring more temporary joy like a new pair of sunglasses or a shirt. Plants will improve the air quality in your space, add to the aesthetic, and perhaps most importantly they will *literally* liven your space. Having living things around your house will raise the vibrational energy level and give you some sense of purpose on the days where getting out of bed feels like climbing Mount Everest barefoot.

These days you don't have to have a green thumb; you can Google "easiest house plants to keep alive" and you'll be greeted with plenty of low-maintenance ideas. Sometimes you need to *create* things that are easy to accomplish, so that you can *find* a sense of accomplishment and purpose in your days when you're feeling low. Watering and tending to your house plants is not a strenuous activity, and doesn't require much time, but could be just the task you need on a day you're feeling hopeless. Akin to gardening, the act of caring for plants is a therapeutic effort that has been shown to positively impact mental health.

Cleanliness is a factor too. Some people actually enjoy cleaning and find it meditative. But, if that's not you, the cleanliness of your space will still affect your well-being, energy and emotions. Being surrounded by filth is a real drag. If you're in the "I *hate* cleaning" category...springing for a cleaning service instead of physical elements for your space may be a game changer for you and well-worth the investment.

Our atmosphere plays a role in how we set ourselves up to get through circumstances where we're craving support.

19. REVEL IN THE MAGIC OF MUSIC.

Music has the ability to alter our mood like nothing else in life. I worked for a non-profit organization right out of college called S.O.U.L (Singers of United Lands) that brought singers from other countries to the United States to perform native music from their home country and teach audiences about their cultures. Part of our mission was that we were bringing education and cultural understanding to people through the one universal language: music.

If you take a minute to think about it, we all have those certain songs; when we hear them they evoke instant emotion, sometimes nostalgia and definite pause. Whether it's attached to a specific memory or the song itself just speaks to you, perhaps through your subconscious; you know without a doubt when it comes on that it'll make you cry or want to dance, bring a smile to your face, give you the motivation to push it to the limit in a workout. *That* is the magic of music and we can use it to our benefit.

A few of my personal go-to's are "Higher Love" (the original, so many of the incredible remixes over the years - any version really - that song gives me goosebumps and makes me want to belt it from the rooftops!), "Silver Lining" by Mt. Joy and "Better People" by Xavier Rudd.

That same little notebook I've suggested in a few of these practices already? Here's another great use for that handy dandy little diary:

When you hear these songs - in a store, in the car, in a commercial, in a show or movie - write them down so you can keep a running list handy. In moments you really need a mood shift, you might not be able to think of them, but if you have a list, you've removed obstacles. Removing obstacles is so important when you're feeling overwhelmed.

Once you have your running list you can take it a step further and make yourself a playlist on Spotify or Pandora or whatever you use for music so you have easy access to press 'play' when you need it most.

On the subject of playlists, borrow playlists or even ask for them! I've been to yoga classes for example where the music was my favorite part of the practice and I started making a habit of asking the instructor afterward if they'd be willing to share the playlist. Many will; I follow my favorite yoga instructor on Spotify so that I can easily access and listen to her epic playlists.

Another example is calling on those you love. We all need help sometimes, but more often than not, we don't know how to ask or what to ask for. I know music is a powerful tool for me and one of my longest, childhood friends has the most beautiful taste in music. Just thinking about being on a roadtrip with her listening to her music puts a smile on my face. I asked her to make me a Spotify playlist. I didn't get too specific, I just said "when you have time, make me a playlist of some of your favorite jams." She did and I'm so grateful. I listen to it all the time. Not only does the music itself lift my spirits, but as a bonus, I feel closer to my friend every time I listen, even though we live thousands of miles apart.

There are also pre-made playlists that can be pretty solid go-to's. I'm most familiar with Spotify because that's what I use, but I'm sure other services offer something similar. Spotify has playlists curated literally by mood and genre - so if you need to try something quick and dirty, try browsing what's already made and out there for you.

There are times when getting quiet with our thoughts can be highly beneficial, and others where we need something to help us snap out of it. Something to help us shift. For those moments, turn on some music instead of coping with your swirling thoughts in silence and let the music soothe your soul.

20. JUST DANCE.

L ook for a piece of research on endorphins and dance and read up if you need some extra validation beyond some stranger telling you to dance ;-)

Hand-in-hand with music, when you let loose and move your body to a beat – whether you have rhythm or not – it boosts your mood, releases endorphins and takes your mind off of everything else in the moment. "Dance like nobody's watching" anybody? There's a reason this is a timeless phrase for encouragement and joy.

Have you ever seen an unhappy person on the dance floor at a wedding? I didn't think so.

Not only does dancing get your body in motion without the structure or pressure of a "workout," but it is a total redirect of the mind. It's hard to move your body to music and still be stuck in your head. This is an activity to move you into your heart space.

Depending on your comfort level, personality and preferences, incorporating some time to dance in your life might mean scheduling a night out to go dancing with friends, or signing up to take a dance class. If this sounds like your worst nightmare, it might mean turning up the tunes and dancing while you're in the shower (careful in the slip zone, no jumps!) or in your kitchen making dinner. You don't have to break out in a full on routine. This could be simply bobbing your head and shaking your booty or rocking the air guitar - in most cases no one will be watching, so the only judgements you need to cast aside are your own.

For me dancing most often happens in the kitchen while I'm cooking. I keep a bluetooth speaker in the kitchen and dance my heart out with my spoon microphone. It's so silly and random. It's truly *difficult* to not smile and laugh, most times regardless of the kind of day I've had.

You can take this idea a step further and tie it into #11 and a daily gratitude practice: I fully understand in our darkest hours even finding a single thing to be grateful for can be a challenge. I've had plenty of days where this felt inauthentic. Where if I were brutally honest, I literally felt grateful for nothing. Here's where the power of choice comes in. Sometimes you *do* have to force it. Our negative thought patterns contribute to overwhelming emotions, and these patterns are subconscious habits. Old habits die hard.

Choose to dance. And you automatically have *something* to be grateful for. The fact you can *hear* the music. The fact your body is *capable* of movement. The magic of these human bodies of ours, and what they allow us to experience in this life is a damn gift each and every day. So if you're grateful for nothing else some days, you can be grateful for that, and dancing will remind you when you've forgotten.

Don't overthink this. Just move to the music.

Dance your heart out.

21. REWARD YOURSELF FOR A CHORE OR TASK WITH SOMETHING OUT OF THE ORDINARY FOR YOU.

In periods of time that are uniquely heavy, it can be hard to find the motivation to do anything; whether you mind it or not, like it or not, really have to do it or not. We all have times where literally everything feels like the equivalent of having to get up in the morning and go to work early for the staff meeting with a hangover. Miserable, right?

A good example for me is grocery shopping. Even on a good day, going grocery shopping is quite possibly my least favorite necessity of life and if I'm not in a good mood, I might choose not eating dinner over going to the store.

When you're working through life's shit and you're dragging to accomplish everyday tasks, you need to break up the monotony with things to remind yourself you're getting through.

So! Pair your dreaded tasks with something that feels like far less of a drag. I started going grocery shopping only when I have a solid few hour window, so I know I will have time to get myself a treat afterward. Once I drop off the groceries and put them away, my personal favorite is going to sit at a cute, independent coffee shop and enjoy an overpriced latte in peace. I made it through grocery shopping, which feeds my family for the week and I deserve it. And so do you! Whatever your treat may be ... don't think of 'treat yo' self' as a joke... put it into practice!

Plan around the reward rather than the task so you have something to look forward to.

22. MAP OUT YOUR WEEK.

W e live in an era of overwhelm, because our society supports and uplifts overwhelming expectations. That is the reality around us. And it's compounded by personal tragedies and hardships; and uncontrollable outside forces, like err, hurricanes or global pandemics.

Everywhere you turn you're being pushed to *go go go, do do do, share share share, achieve achieve achieve, buy buy buy, advance advance advance.* While there's nothing wrong with ambition, or bettering ourselves or setting big goals – there is something inherently disconnected about the way we have come to characterize "priorities." On top of that, sometimes shit hits the proverbial fan, despite our best efforts to avoid it!

> *Relax, <u>nothing</u> is under control. (<<<That's probably the best advice I have ever received.)*

Once upon a time I wrote this Thought Catalog article about priorities, and it's worth a read (not just because I wrote it).

Ever had a meeting with your boss about being overwhelmed and trying to figure out how you're going to get it all done and they say, "you just need to prioritize." Or vented to your significant other about how exhausted you are and you don't know how you're going to get it all done and they say, "you just need to figure out what your priorities are."

THAT'S THE PROBLEM! **Priority** was never meant to be pluralized and multiplied. You can't prioritize *everything* otherwise "priority" becomes completely and utterly meaningless.

Put your foot down, with everyone around you, and make it clear that you have **a few** clearly defined priorities and they **will** take precedence over anything else. Period.

On Sunday nights I started outlining my weekly priorities by breaking them down into 4 categories. Of course this may be different for everyone, but I'll share what I do as an example to give you context.

Work, Home, Us (meaning my husband and I), Me. In each of these categories, I identify ONLY 3-4 things in each category I plan to address or tackle for the week and if I can make it to all of them I know my week will have felt like a success. Some of these priorities are big and some are very small. They range usually from actual tasks to maybe having a conversation or doing something that qualifies as self care in the "me" category.

Before I address emails in the morning, or even think about any of the million other random things that come up on a daily basis, I refer to my weekly list and look at what kind of time I could carve out each day to dedicate toward these clearly defined priorities.

Part of working through overwhelm is eliminating noise. And sometimes that means saying 'no' to other people or saying 'no' to doing. Being comfortable sticking to your guns in this way can be very difficult and even feel unnatural. What makes it a little easier is having clearly outlined priorities and knowing whatever additional thing is being asked of you doesn't fit. Remember too, you may not always be delivering a flat out "no," but saying "unfortunately I don't have the bandwidth, but I could address that next week (in two weeks, etc.)" or "I can't help you do that, but what I could do is..." Blame your priorities instead of beating yourself over not being able to be the 'yes' person.

Breaking your week up by category also helps to remind you one area of life is not more important than the other. Especially when your mental health is suffering, it helps to identify that just as important as your job or taking care of your family or home, your mental health and taking care of yourself is deserving of a category all its own.

Even if your categories are different than mine, make sure you adopt the "me" category.

23. VISUAL REMINDERS OF WHAT YOU'RE WORKING TOWARDS.

A vision board is not a new concept, and certainly not one I came up with, but I have found great value in loud, in-my-face visual reminders of what I'm working toward especially in periods of time where I felt down and out. This could look very different depending on where you're at and what you're working toward.

Shortly after my Mom passed away, I made a mini vision board on the back of a file folder and hung it on my fridge for several months to look at everyday. It was filled with words and visual cues for comfort and healing I was seeking. Things like "acceptance," "connection," "hope." It was also filled with physical goals. Working out was paramount for me during my early grieving process. For a good while, being at the gym was the only time of day I didn't feel numb. And so I gave myself physical goals to focus on like getting better at double unders and achieving muscle ups (shout out to all my fellow CrossFitters!). Those were on the vision board. And food related goals too. I needed as many reminders as I could muster to take care of myself at a time when the basics would have been very easy to neglect.

If you're grieving, going through a health crisis, dealing with an unexpected career change, going through a parenting challenge; whatever the case may be, you may be so overwhelmed you feel your ability to work toward your greater life goals is being negatively impacted. First and foremost, while it's important to our own evolution to identify goals to work towards, it's equally important to recognize that our goals can be fluid. They may need to pause or adjust given our circumstances. We need to be open to the ebb and flow of life and the inevitable unexpected, whilst still maintaining a reason to keep pushing forward. Otherwise, what's the point of going through the motions?

Feeling like our goals have been put on hold or thrown off track will give us another reason to beat ourselves up and wallow in self misery if we allow it to.

For both my husband and I, we're heavily goal oriented, so in our house we took the visual cues to a whole new level. We painted an entire wall of our home office with chalkboard paint and covered the whole wall with our goals, visions, and plans for 2020. We make an effort to read it everyday

We're due for an update since the outbreak of COVID-19. As I said, goals, even when written on the wall, need to be fluid to accommodate *life.* Ya feel me? #2020

Being business owners during this strange moment in history has been one of the most stressful periods of our life together. Some of our goals and plans this year have been dramatically impacted as a result of circumstances completely out of our control. It doesn't change the fact that everyday, when we look at that wall - we're reminded of our big dreams. Reminded of *why* we do what we do. Reminded of what we're working toward when the monotony of the everyday grind gets to be a lot to bear.

When we're feeling hopeless, frustrated, confused, angry...we need to be reminded of possibility. We need to be reminded of hope, and health and happiness. We need to be reminded of what we're capable of. And what we're capable of is only limited by our dreams and goals and plans and the actions they inspire us to take. The first step is holding yourself accountable, even when the original "plan" gets a bit jumbled by life. Remind yourself visually, you can get back on track.

24. CONNECT WITH NATURE.

When you're feeling disconnected. From life as you "knew" it, from yourself, from others, from clarity...it's vitally important to connect with nature.

Even simple things like making the decision to get up and go for a walk outside for 15 minutes each day can make a huge difference. Removing yourself from exposure to blue light from screens and the constant buzz of things like air conditioners or refrigerators is important to clear the mind and give the body a chance to ground. Not to mention you need to get some fresh air!

If you're struggling through depression, severe anxiety, grief or sadness - any form of emotional overwhelm - the desire to curl up in a ball and hide from the world can take a stronghold on you. In our increasingly digital world, not to mention the current deterrents raining down on our society to try and encourage social isolation and "staying home" as much as possible; for many, the option to not leave the house actually now exists. This can be startlingly detrimental to your emotional well-being. Take it from someone who has worked from home for several years now - I have fallen into ruts where I didn't leave the house for days and it wreaked havoc on both my body and mind.

Above and beyond the basic benefits of spending time out-doors, there's a deeper benefit to connecting with nature. There are many ways to make efforts to strengthen your connection but one of the easiest I've found is to go out and find a place to sit comfortably where you have a view of a really beautiful plant or tree. Set the timer on your phone, or simply check your watch. And sit. For 15 minutes, stare at the tree or plant. Take note of the veins of stems, the patterns of bark, the way the leaves move in the wind. Observe the plant or tree with your full attention and focus. This will bring you incredible clarity around the divine wisdom of nature. It teaches us to appreciate patience physically (we're a society that has forgotten how to sit still), by doing something we might otherwise consider odd, "boring," or a waste of time. And you will feel an enhanced level of connectivity to the natural environment by taking the time for this simple, but powerful observation.

Emotionally, by observing the intricacies of the plant we're focusing on, we can also almost instantly feel the integration of a *philosophy of patience* into our perspective as well. How many years do you think it took for the tree to grow that tall? How did nature perfectly design that tree to withstand the weather? How is it that the tree or plant inherently grew in such a way to provide shelter and be a food source for other animals and insects?

I have found taking the time to spend with nature and ponder these types of questions has brought me back time and time again to a place of understanding. A place of understanding that the natural order and evolution of every living thing including ourselves is centered around *patience.* That the life cycle of all beings and plants is a *process.* That everything is designed perfectly in the natural world around us as well as within us.

Being outside listening to the sounds of nature; be it the chirping of birds, the washing of waves, the wind in the trees, does something else for me too. It reminds me we are all but a spec. Not in the sense of minimizing our experience; there's no doubt we all go through real, gut-wrenching pain and struggle. But in the sense that, no matter what's going on with us, the world is still turning. Above and beyond the billions of other people with their own unique lives playing out, every ant, bird, dolphin, etc. is also on *its* own journey through life and it doesn't stop regardless of our personal experience. It's a humbling reminder that our life is bigger and holds more than our hardships (even if they feel all consuming in the moment), and that time will not stand still. *Every moment in time, no matter how difficult, will pass.*

25. FIND A THERAPIST.

I wanted to save this one for last because I know it looks and sounds and feels loaded. Depending upon your life experience and the way you've been conditioned to think, feel and talk about mental health, talking to a therapist may sound like exactly what you need, or it may sound like the most uncomfortable, wackadoodle idea you've ever heard.

Therapy also does not feel accessible to everyone. It can be very expensive, it's rarely covered by insurance, and if you've never gone to therapy before, figuring out where to even *look* for said therapist might feel completely overwhelming in itself.

I am a huge proponent of therapy. It has been monumentally helpful for me in my life and I truly believe every human being on the planet, overwhelmed or not, could benefit from a neutral, third party listening ear and the chance to take in a completely unbiased perspective. You *know* how conflicting your internal voices can be. I believe it's essential for humans to have a resource outside of themselves to process all that is life and the way our brains perceive it.

As far as looking for a therapist; in my early twenties after breaking away from an abusive relationship I began looking for my first therapist. I had no idea what I was doing and my Mom suggested asking my primary care doctor for a recommendation. I called and asked if they had therapists they referred out to and they gave me a few names and numbers. The first one with an available appointment that week was the one I booked. Luckily she was actually a really great fit for me and what I was going through and I saw her once a week for the next two years.

Since then, in moving to different places and moving through different stages, I've explored therapy and run into the scenario where I just didn't click with the therapist. I always heed this warning to people: while your therapist is someone you're hiring, they are still human and you are going to be forming a type of relationship with them, so not every therapist will be helpful to you. It should be approached as a process and it's okay if the first therapist you go to doesn't feel like a great fit.

On the same token, therapists need a chance to get to know you beyond your current situation. They need a chance to dive into your background and history, and yes, your childhood, to really begin to understand you and the life experience you're operating from. Your complete life experience has a huge impact on your current emotional battles and the way you react to life circumstances. So while it's okay to be in the mindset of searching for the right therapist, be prepared to give someone several sessions for an adequate chance to dive in. If after that you *still* feel they're not a great fit or there's not much progress being made, consider moving on to the next.

It took you a lifetime to build up your defense machanisms and develop your emotional thought patterns and habits. Even the most qualified therapist will not be able to wave their magic wand and solve all your problems in an hour. Cultivate patience.

Another helpful resource for finding a therapist is Psychology Today. They have a directory you can use to search therapists by location, but also by speciality, modality, price, what insurance they accept, and even things like gender and age if you feel strongly about needing to relate to this person on a specific demographic level.

In the era of COVID-19 and an accelerated push to digitize what we haven't already, I've also seen a surge in telehealth specifically in the mental health space. Lots of different services have popped up and are aimed at making therapy more accessible. While I haven't had any personal experience with the service, I've seen a lot of buzz around Better Help for example which offers online counseling and has plans starting at $40 a week in addition to financial aid you can apply for according to their website. I'm sure there are other similar services out there like it.

Therapy can be scary. We live in a society that sadly still clings to a major stigma around mental health.

Here's my two cents: if you're in a dark place and have come to the realization you don't know how to help yourself, what's the harm in trying? You are worth it.

BONUS!

L imit your social media use in times of deep despair. Overwhelm is one thing. When it compounds into more serious symptoms and forms: depression, intrusive thoughts, disordered eating...all of the above...you need to take action to protect your heart and mind. For me I've done this many times over the years. Sometimes I do it for a day, sometimes a week, sometimes a month.

How do I know it's time for a social media detox? Usually when I'm most drawn to it. If you find yourself feeling so awful you can't bring yourself to do anything but scroll just to pass the time...it's probably time for a break.

Why? First, that #filterlife. Social media has become largely focused on two things: sharing all the highlights of our lives while omitting all the other stuff. Or debating highly controversial topics with no interest at all in understanding or meaningful conversation. BOTH of which will only make you feel worse when you're already down.

Beyond that, there's something deeply, psychologically disturbing about the way social media has developed. You may think you're simply scrolling your feed checking in on your friends, family and favorite celebrities - being served the occasional ad. But social media's algorithms have become so sophisticated they are literally controlling *everything* you see based on *your* current situation. Your mood, your habits, what your behavioral tendencies are.

If you've never delved into this at all, at risk of scaring the proverbial shit out of you, I highly recommend watching The Social Dilemma on Netflix if that's available to you; or at the very least doing some reading around the subject matter of the film. Basically: these tech companies know exactly how to not only determine, but *play* to your current mood and emotional state, and serve you content that you tend to gravitate to when in a particular state; content that will play to your *weaknesses*.

Take an intentional break and focus instead on being present in your life and experimenting with some of the suggestions in this book, or other resources you have found helpful in the past. For me, when I decide I'm taking a break - I typically will post something letting people know I am doing so, mainly for the purpose of holding myself accountable. But if you're worried about your own level of self control and being able to steer clear you could go as far as moving these apps off of the home screen of your phone, or one step further, temporarily uninstalling the apps all together. You can always reinstall when you're ready to rejoin the digital sphere.

I don't believe social media is evil. I quite like it actually (most of the time); especially Instagram, it's my favorite. I'm a pretty picture junky. But, once I started consciously observing my moods in relation to my social media usage, I became very aware of how it can negatively impact me at times. Knowing when to take a break has been a game changer.

BONUS BONUS: ON GRIEF.

I f you are grieving right now. Grieving the loss of a loved one. Grieving the loss of a job. Grieving a relationship. Heck, grieving the world as we once knew it and the current state of social and political turmoil and upheaval...

Honor your grief. Recognize it. Call it by name. Talk about it. Let those around you know what you're going through.

Perhaps most importantly, and something it took me several soul-shaking losses to understand: grief is NOT a linear journey with a beginning, middle and end. Yes there are stages of grief we all experience. But what I've learned is that grief is actually a continuous cycle. Once you've been met with a life experience that leads to grief, it nevers leaves you, it becomes **a part of you**. It becomes a part of the fabric of your life's journey and helps shape your evolution as a human being. Grief is not always sobbing on the bathroom floor and not being able to get out of bed.

Certainly, grief becomes easier to cope with over time. With time to process and integrate, you begin to see your losses with a different perspective than you once did. But, grief never leaves you. It's never over. There will not be a time where you are "over it." In my experience this is one of the most painful societal false pretenses there is.

Do not let ANYONE put a timeline on your grief. Do not let ANYONE impart their opinion on when you should be "ready." Ready to talk, ready to go back to work or school, ready to do this or that, ready to put the tears away, ready to put on a smile and let the world know you're "done" healing...

Don't get me wrong; I don't want you to be stuck in a

portion of your grief cycle making your experience more painful than it needs to be. That's a huge reason I've written this book - to share some of my own experiences and some of the things that have helped me through.

But I do want to give you permission. Permission you may not be feeling from anyone else in your life. Permission I know I felt I didn't always have. Permission to feel the way you feel and know your journey is completely unique.

I want to give you confidence too. Confidence that while your grief will serve you some of your most painful days, at some point it will also become one of your greatest strengths. It will become a tool. It will become your empathy and compassion. It will become your perception of life and what it all means. It will make you a better person. It will always be a part of you; just in different shapes and forms at different times.

Lean into your grief journey and follow your own damn timeline.

PARTING THOUGHTS...

I'm so honored. Honored you bought this book or someone bought it for you. Honored to share space and time with you. And humbled that if you've read to this point, you felt my words worthy enough of your time and attention.

My hope in putting this out into the world, and sharing some brief snippets of my own journey I've never shared before has been for one purpose: Despite all I've experienced and the tools I've discovered, the year 2020 knocked me off of my feet. I hit some of the lowest emotional points of my life in 2020. It was the first time I related on a visceral level to some of the intrusive thoughts I used to watch my Mom battle. The type of thoughts I knew were painful and serious, but didn't really "get."

The state of our world and the heavy energy of our collective population, combined with trying to run and operate multiple businesses in the midst of a global pandemic, perfectly prodded many of my deepest fears. And things got dark.

I found myself thinking: If I feel this way, with all the tools and resources at my disposal and the incredible support network I'm so blessed to have, how must other people be feeling? What must other people be going through?

If my words and ideas can help even one person pick themselves up, shift their energy, pivot, try something new...if one person takes one little nugget away from this that helps them in some way, this will have been worth it.

That's my deepest hope and desire and I'd love if that person were YOU.

I'll offer one more small musing; something I shared on the one-year anniversary of my Mother's death that is so raw for me and has been oh-so-applicable many times over:

There will be things that happen in this life you're sure will break you. But then you look up and realize a year has gone by; and not only did you survive, but if you're lucky - you've ended up with a bigger, deeper understanding of what it's all for. And that's where the peace comes. Doesn't mean you don't have to look for it some days, but it's there if you're willing to love, let go, learn and grow.

For my friends reading in the United States, if you are struggling with intrusive thoughts, or in the deepest depths of despair feeling like there's nowhere left to turn, please know there are crisis resources available to you; I have listed several on the next page. For international readers, I urge you to be proactive in researching the phone numbers or websites of services like this in your home country so you have them should you ever need them. You are loved, you are worthy and you are deserving of help and healing <3

US CRISIS RESOURCES

Emergency: 911

National Domestic Violence Hotline: 1- 800-799-7233

National Suicide Prevention Lifeline: 1-800-273-TALK (8255)

National Hopeline Network: 1-800-SUICIDE (800-784-2433)

Crisis Text Line: Text "DESERVE" TO 741-741

Lifeline Crisis Chat (Online live messaging): https://suicidepreventionlifeline.org/chat/

Self-Harm Hotline: 1-800-DONT CUT (1-800-366-8288)

Planned Parenthood Hotline: 1-800-230-PLAN (7526)

American Association of Poison Control Centers: 1-800-222-1222

National Council on Alcoholism & Drug Dependency Hope Line: 1-800-622-2255

National Crisis Line - Anorexia and Bulimia: 1-800-233-4357

GLBT Hotline: 1-888-843-4564

TREVOR Crisis Hotline: 1-866-488-7386

AIDS Crisis Line: 1-800-221-7044

Veterans Crisis Line: https://www.veteranscrisisline.net

TransLifeline: https://www.translifeline.org - 877-565-8860

Suicide Prevention Wiki: http://suicideprevention.wikia.com

Made in the USA
Monee, IL
01 December 2020

50435498R00073